101 words every grown-up should know

101 words every grown-up should know

Essential definitions for every educated vocabulary

Linda J. Beam

SWEETWATER
PRESS

SWEETWATER
PRESS

101 Words Every Grown-up Should Know

Copyright © 2007 by Cliff Road Books, Inc.

Produced by arrangement with Sweetwater Press

ISBN-13: 978-1-58173-718-9
ISBN-10: 1-58173-718-1

A New Look at Old Skills

Remember those dull vocabulary tests you had every week when you were in school? You'd memorize the words and their definitions long enough to get through the test, and then you'd forget them. You thought you'd never need them again.

As an adult, you know better. Now you realize that words are power, and the more you know, the more able you are to express yourself clearly and precisely. Because good communications skills are so valuable in the workplace, not to mention in your personal conversations, they can pay off in many ways.

It's more than that, too. People often judge us by the words we use. You can either make solid word choices that convey exact meanings, or lazy ones. Make good choices and you send a positive message about yourself. Choose words that are overused and your message may not get the attention you hope for. It's up to you.

101 Words Every Grown-up Should Know presents words that will be useful in your business and personal life. Flip through its pages and you'll find not only easy-to-understand definitions, but also a simple pronunciation guide, plus sample sentences to show how each word is correctly used.

Use the proper words confidently with the help of this conveniently sized, readable volume. Brushing up on your vocabulary has never been easier.

1. Aberrant [ab-er-rant]

Noun
> Any person or thing that differs substantially from the norm: *John was the aberrant in the test group.*

Adjective
> Deviating from the norm; abnormal; exceptional; atypical: *His aberrant behavior was the first symptom that something was wrong.*

Related words: *Nouns* – aberrance, aberrancy
                 Adverb – aberrantly

Synonyms: abnormal, anomalous, deviant, divergent, irregular, unusual

Antonyms: normal, ordinary, same, traditional, usual

> **"I tend to be drawn to the more aberrant characters. There's more to do with them."**
> **- Robert Tunney**

2. Abscond [ab-**scond**]

Verb

To run away, often quickly or suddenly, in order to avoid being discovered: *The oldest son tried to abscond with several family treasures.*

Related words: *Noun* – absconder
Verbs – absconded, absconding, absconds

Synonyms: bolt, flee

Antonyms: abide, endure, remain, stay

"When the angels present themselves, the devils abscond."
– Arabic Proverb

3. Acquiesce [ac-qui-**esce**]

Verb
> To comply, submit, or yield to something or someone without protest; to agree: *The prosecuting attorney was asked to acquiesce on several points of law.*

Related words: *Noun* – acquiescence
Verb – acquiescing
Adverb – acquiescingly

Synonyms: assent, comply, give in

Antonyms: disagree, dissent, object, protest, resist

> **"The strongest and most effective force in guaranteeing the long-term maintenance of power is not violence in all the forms deployed by the dominant to control the dominated, but consent in all the forms in which the dominated acquiesce in their own domination."**
> **– Robert Frost**

4. Acumen [ac-u-men]

Noun
> Keen insight or judgment; unusual
> discernment: *Margaret's business acumen was
> finally rewarded with a promotion.*

Related words: *Noun* – acumination
                 Adjective – acuminate

Synonyms: ability, astuteness, discrimination,
    knowledge, savvy, sharpness, shrewdness

Usage: Historically, acumen has been pronounced
    with stress on the second syllable. Modern
    usage, however, allows for emphasis on the
    first syllable.

5. Acute [a-**cute**]

Adjective

Sharp or severe; especially pronounced: *The patient described acute pain in his back.*

Sensitive to details or impressions: *John was an acute observer of human nature.*

In geometry, an angle less than 90 degrees: *Jessie did not match the acute angle with the correct answer.*

In music terminology, high in pitch or shrill: *The music had several acute pitches in the solo part.*

Noun

An accent mark placed above a vowel to aid pronunciation: *The acute accent caused a problem for some students.*

Related words: *Noun* – acuteness
               Adverb – acutely

Synonyms: astute, bright, clever, keen, perceptive, sharp-witted, smart, wise

"He alone is an acute observer, who can observe minutely without being observed."
– Johann Kaspar Lavater

6. Ambiguous [am-**big**-u-ous]

Adjective

Unclear: *John offered an ambiguous explanation for his tardiness.*

Having several possible meanings or interpretations: *The poem had an ambiguous meaning.*

Related words: *Nouns* – ambiguity, ambiguousness
Adverb – ambiguously

Synonyms: cloudy, cryptic, enigmatic, equivocal, nebulous, obscure, uncertain, vague

Antonyms: clear, defined, definite, explicit, lucid

7. Anachronism [a-**nach**-ro-nism]

Noun

A person or thing that seems to be out of its natural time or place; something outdated: *The typewriter is an anachronism in modern business settings.*

Related words: *Adjectives* – anachronistic, anachronous
Adverbs – anachronically, anachronistically, anachronously

8. Apt [apt]

Adjective

Likely to do a certain thing: *The toddler is apt to run into the street if not watched carefully.*

Particularly fitting or precise: *The pastor always has an apt response when asked about scriptures.*

Having an unusual potential for learning: *Sarah was known to be an apt pupil in all her classes.*

Related words: *Noun* – aptness
Adverb – aptly

Synonyms: adroit, felicitous, fitting, germane, liable, meet, pertinent, skillful,

> **"Among all kinds of writing, there is none in which Authors are more apt to miscarry than in works of Humour, as there is none in which they are more ambitious to excel."**
> **- Joseph Addison**

9. Arcane [ar-**cane**]

Adjective

Known to just a few: *Jonathan's comments revealed knowledge of several arcane disciplines.*

Obscure: *An arcane language was used for the code.*

Synonyms: cabalistic, enigmatic, mysterious

> "Art is a step from what is obvious and well-known toward what is arcane and concealed."
> – Kahlil Gibran

10. Assuage [as-**suage**]

Verb

> To lessen: *Eldred visited the cemetery every day to try to assuage his grief.*

> To satisfy: *The lost boys ate quickly to assuage their hunger.*

> To calm: *The child's mother held him tightly to assuage his fears.*

Related words: *Nouns* – assuagement, assuager

Synonyms: allay, alleviate, ease, lighten, mitigate, relieve

Antonyms: intensify

"I pray that our heavenly Father may assuage the anguish of your bereavement, and leave you only the cherished memory of the loved and lost, and the solemn pride that must be yours to have laid so costly a sacrifice upon the altar of freedom."
- Letter from Abraham Lincoln to Mrs. Bixby, November 21, 1864

11. Banal [ba-**nal**]

Adjective
Lacking originality; commonplace: *Joe's paper offered a banal look at King Arthur's court.*

Related words: *Noun* – banality
Verb – banalize
Adverb – banally

Synonyms: hackneyed, ordinary, pedestrian, stale, stereotypic, tired, trite, worn-out

Antonyms: fresh, new, original, uncommon, unparalleled, unique

Usage: There are currently several common pronunciations of this word. All are considered to be acceptable.

> **"No soap opera has so engrossingly captured the wondrous banality of the human condition."**
> **– Harry F. Waters**

12. Brusque (also brusk) [brusque]

Adjective
Abrupt; blunt: *Todd gave a brusque answer to his mother's inquiries.*

Related words: *Noun* – brusqueness
                 Adverb – brusquely

Synonyms: crusty, curt, gruff, short

Antonyms: courteous, kind, patient, long-suffering, tactful

13. Cajole [ca-**jole**]

Verb

To persuade; to urge repeatedly, often with flattery: *Jamie planned to cajole her mother into letting her go to the party.*

Related words: *Nouns* – cajolement, cajoler
Adverb – cajolingly

Synonyms: coax, sweet-talk, wheedle

It is estimated that the average educated person knows about 20,000 words.

14. Castigate [cas-ti-gate]

Verb

To criticize or rebuke severely: *The mayor castigated the councilman for his stand on the proposed legislation.*

To punish: *She castigated the newsman for his insensitive question.*

Related words: *Nouns* – castigation, castigator
Adjectives – castigative, castigatory

Synonyms: admonish, chasten, chastise, chide, correct, discipline, reprimand, reprove, scold, upbraid

Antonyms: praise, reward

"In 1979, I was castigated for asking Senator Edward Kennedy on a CBS News documentary about the state of his marriage."
- Roger Mudd

15. Catalyst [cat-a-lyst]

Noun

A person or thing that causes a reaction without being affected itself: *The speech was a catalyst for change in the organization.*

In chemistry, a substance that prompts or accelerates a chemical reaction without suffering any effect itself: *The acid was just the catalyst needed to make the mixture explode.*

Synonyms: agent, facilitator

"Painful as it may be, a significant emotional event can be the catalyst for choosing a direction that serves us—and those around us—more effectively. Look for the learning."
- Louisa May Alcott

16. Caustic [**caus**-tic]

Adjective

Abrasive; capable of burning or corroding: *The acid had a caustic effect on the gloves worn by the professor.*

Bitter: *The spurned lover's caustic comments revealed his hurt.*

Related words: *Nouns* – causticity, causticness
Adverbs – caustically, causticly

Synonyms: biting, corrosive, cutting, sarcastic, scathing, sharp, stinging, vitriolic

Antonyms: encouraging, reassuring, soothing

17. Caveat [**ca**-ve-at]

Noun

A warning or admonition: *The store's owner gave his managers free reign, with a caveat to use authority wisely.*

A legal notice: *The attorney filed a caveat against the probate of Mr. Johnson's will.*

Related words: *Verbs* – caveated, caveatting

18. Chronic [chron-ic]

Adjective
>Recurring, constant: *Tony's back pain was chronic.*

>Of long duration: *The small country was in a chronic state of turmoil.*

Related words: *Noun* – chronicity
>*Adverb* – chronically

Synonyms: confirmed, continuing, habitual, inveterate, lingering, persistent

Antonyms: intermittent, occasional, periodic

19. Circumspect [cir-cum-spect]

Adjective
Cautious; prudent; careful; guarded: *As a new employee, Ken was circumspect about his behavior and comments.*

Related words: *Noun* – circumspectness
　　　　　　　　Adverb – circumspectly

Synonyms: careful, conservative, prudent, wary, vigilant

Antonyms: careless, indiscreet, loose

"Be very circumspect in the choice of thy company."
-   Francis Quarles

20. Concurrent [con-**cur**-rent]

Adjective

Occurring at the same time: *The verdict called for two concurrent penalties.*

In agreement: *The concurrent efforts of two groups brought about the change.*

Having equal authority: *The concurrent committees produced a successful event.*

Intersecting at a common point: *Four concurrent lines formed the design.*

Related word: *Adverb* – concurrently

Synonyms: coexistent, coincident, contemporaneous, contemporary, simultaneous, together

Antonym: separate

21. Consecutive [con-**sec**-u-tive]

Adjective
> One following another in an uninterrupted progression: *Those holding the office were limited to two consecutive terms.*

Related words: *Noun* – consecutiveness
                Adverb – consecutively

Synonyms: continuous, sequential, serial, subsequent, successive

---

New words are often created from new concepts, events, or inventions within a society. New words, terms, or phrases are called neologisms, a term that was coined around 1800. An example of a neologism would be ezine, which is a periodic publication such as a newsletter that is distributed electronically.

22. Copious [co-pi-ous]

Adjective
> Abundant; plentiful: *I can never decide what to do with my copious leisure time.*

Related words: *Nouns* – copiosity, copiousness
                 Adverb – copiously

Synonyms: ample, bounteous, bountiful, generous, plenteous, substantial, voluminous

Antonyms: inadequate, insufficient, meager, scanty, scarce

> **"Dylan talked copiously, then stopped. 'Somebody's boring me,' he said, 'I think it's me.'"**
> **– Dylan Thomas**

23. Corroborate [cor-**rob-o-rate**]

Verb

    To confirm or agree with: *The other witness corroborated my account of the accident.*

Related words: *Noun* – corroborator
                     Adjective – corroboratory
                     Adverbs – corroboratively,
                        corroboratorily

Synonyms: back up, endorse, substantiate, validate, verify

Antonyms: contradict, deny, disallow, refute, reject

24. Culpable [**cul**-pa-ble]

Adjective
   At fault; deserving blame: *Jack's wreckless actions made him culpable in the incident.*

Related words: *Nouns* – culpability, culpableness
                    Adverb – culpably

Synonyms: blameworthy, guilty

Antonyms: innocent

---

25. Cumulative [**cu**-mu-la-tive]

Adjective
   Increasing in successive amounts; adding gradually as you proceed: *The benefits of eating properly are cumulative.*

Related words: *Noun* – cumulativeness
                    Adverb – cumulatively

Synonyms: accumulative, additive

26. Dearth [dearth]

Noun

A lack of; an inadequate supply of: *There was a dearth of qualified applicants for the specialized position.*

Synonyms: inadequacy, insufficiency, paucity, shortage

Antonyms: abundance, bountiful, excess, plenty, surplus

"A field needs to keep growing and changing if it's going to maintain its vitality, and I was worried by the dearth of younger writers and editors with any real vision. In the last few years, however, I've been astonished by the number of new people who have been published who are really good."
- Terri Windling

27. Deference [**def**-er-ence]

Noun
> Respectful consideration for; submission or yielding to the judgment of another: *In deference to the bride's wishes, both mothers wore blue.*

Synonyms: acquiescence, agreement, amenability, civility, compliance, honor, obedience, respect, submission

Antonyms: contempt, disobedience, disregard, noncompliance

> **"I am tired of submitting my will to the caprices of others; of resigning my own judgment in deference to those to whom I owe no duty, and for whom I feel no respect."**
> **- From *Lady Susan* by Jane Austen**

28. Deploy [de-**ploy**]

Verb

>To spread out to form a more substantial area of coverage: *Ground forces were deployed during the subsequent attack.*

>To send out or put in position for use: *The plane could not deploy its landing gear for the emergency landing.*

Related words: *Nouns* – deployability, deployer, deployment
Adjective – deployable

Synonyms: arrange, marshal, order, organize

Antonyms: gather

Usage: Although deploy has its origin in military terms, it is now commonly used to describe the distribution and installation of computer applications and programs. In particular, multiple installations of a particular program within a given corporate setting is referred to as deploying applications rather than installing each one individually.

29. Deride [de-**ride**]

Verb

To scorn or taunt: *Seth derided his mother's attempts to make him come home early.*

Related words: *Noun* – derider
Adverb – deridingly

Synonyms: banter, flout, jeer, ridicule

30. Diatribe [**di**-a-tribe]

Noun

Abusive attack, criticism, or ranting: *Professor Rice's diatribe on tardiness made little impact on the students.*

Synonyms: denouncement, fit, harangue, rant, tirade

Antonyms: praise, recommendation

31. Dire [dire]

Adjective

Ominous; predicting terrible consequences:
*Financial forecasts offer dire predictions for
next year.*

Desperate: *Most victims of the hurricane were
in dire need of shelter.*

Related words: *Noun* – direness
                 Adverb – direly

Synonyms: acute, critical, crucial, imperative,
persistent, pressing

Antonyms: fortunate, wonderful

**"Save our nation from the dire
consequences of a prolonged crisis."
-   Joseph Estrada**

32. Disparage [dis-**par**-age]

Verb

> To belittle: *Do not disparage his attempts to better himself.*

> To demean: *Neal spoke in a disparaging manner about the project.*

Related words: *Nouns* – disparagement, disparager
                 Adverb – *disparagingly*

Synonyms: denounce, discredit, mock, ridicule

Antonym: praise

> **"People disparage knowing and the intellectual life, and urge doing. I am content with knowing, if only I could know."**
> **– Ralph Waldo Emerson**

33. Dogmatic [dog-**mat**-ic]

Adjective

Presenting opinions in an arrogant manner; opinionated: *Scott's dogmatic attitude made him an unpleasant coworker.*

Concerning or relating to dogma; doctrinal: *The preacher's sermon was dogmatic.*

Related words: *Noun* – dogmaticalness
Adverb – dogmatically

Synonyms: bossy, dictatorial, domineering, overbearing

Antonyms: doubtful, dubious, equivocal, indecisive, uncertain, vacillating

> **"A teacher who is not dogmatic is simply a teacher who is not teaching."**
> **- Gilbert K. Chesterton**

34. Eclectic [ec-**lec**-tic]

Adjective
Being derived form a variety of sources: *The program included an eclectic selection of music.*

Related word: *Adverb* – electically

Synonyms: broad, catholic, diverse, inclusive, universal, varied

Antonyms: limited, narrow, restrictive, specialized

35. Efficacy [**ef**-fi-ca-cy]

Noun
Effectiveness; ability to produce a desired effect: *The vaccine's efficacy was never in question.*

Synonyms: effectiveness, potency, usefulness

Antonyms: inefficiency, uselessness, weakness

36. Egregious [e-**gre**-gious]

Adjective
Outrageous; extreme in a negative way: *Sue made several egregious mistakes in her presentation.*

Related words: *Noun* – egregiousness
                          Adverb – egregiously

Synonyms: atrocious, extreme, flagrant, glaring, gross, outrageous, remarkable, shocking, striking

Antonyms: insignificant, little, minor, slight, subtle

There's a word to describe the inability to think of the word you need. It's called lethologica.

37. Elated [e-**lat**-ed]

Adjective
Extremely happy: *The parents-to-be were elated to learn they were having twins.*

Related words: *Nouns* – elatedness, elation
Verb – elate
Adverb – elatedly

Synonyms: ecstatic, euphoric, happy, overjoyed, proud, uplifted

Antonyms: dejected, depressed, sad, unhappy

38. Empathy [em-pa-thy]

Noun

Identification with feelings of another person; understanding of another's situation: *Feeling empathy for her sister's loss, Jane began to cry.*

Related words: *Adjective* – empathetic

Synonyms: commiseration, compassion, condolence, pity, sympathy

Antonyms: apathetic, indifference, unfeeling

"The great gift of human beings is that we have the power of empathy."
- Meryl Streep

39. Emulate [em-u-late]

Verb

To imitate; to strive to match or equal: *The preschool students tried to emulate the actions of the older children.*

Related words: *Noun* – emulator
Adjective – emulative
Adverb – emulatively

Synonyms: copy, impersonate, match, mimic, reproduce

> **"My favorite singer to this day is Nat King Cole. I've tried to emulate his phrasing. It is so absolutely beautiful to listen to his lovely voice."**
> **- Johnny Mathis**

40. Epiphany [e-**piph**-a-ny]

Noun

Sudden insight into the meaning of a situation or experience: *Nate's epiphany helped him understand the actions of his family.*

A manifestation, especially of a deity: *The epiphany was witnessed by many faithful followers.*

A Christian festival commemorating the manifestation of Christ to the Gentiles in the persons of the Magi: *The Epiphany is celebrated on June 6.*

Related words: *Adjectives* – epiphanic, epiphanous

41. Erudite [er-u-dite]

Adjective

Having the characteristics of being learned or scholarly: *Sam was often envied for his erudite manner of speaking.*

Related words: *Nouns* – eruditeness, erudition
                 Adverb – eruditely

Synonyms: educated, knowledgeable, wise

Antonyms: common, ignorant, uneducated, unlearned

"Master and Doctor are my titles; for ten years now, without repose, I held my erudite recitals and led my pupils by the nose."
–   Johann Wolfgang von Goethe

42. Esoteric [es-o-**ter**-ic]

Adjective

Understood by or appealing to just a select few with special knowledge: *The poet's esoteric references posed problems for many readers.*

Not publicly disclosed; secret: *The meeting concerned several esoteric matters.*

Related words: *Adverb* – esoterically

Synonyms: abstruse, arcane, deep, profound, recondite

"Poetry can bridge that gap between what is solid and what is suggested; poetry can pull cogent meaning from the vaporous illusions of the esoteric."
- Bryant H. McGill

43. Exacerbate [ex-**ac**-er-bate]

Verb

To increase the severity or intensity of; to make worse: *Alice's tears only exacerbated the situation.*

Related words: *Noun* – exacerbation
Adverb – exacerbatingly

Synonyms: aggravate, intensify, inflame, worsen

Antonyms: alleviate, heal, lessen, relieve, soothe

> "Violent statements and threats cannot provide a solution to the problem. They can only exacerbate feeling and make a clash of forces inevitable."
> - Stafford Cripps

44. Exculpate [ex-cul-pate]

Verb
>To clear from blame; to vindicate: *The parents of the troubled teen were determined to exculpate the young man.*

Related words: *Noun* – exculpation
>*Adjective* – exculpable

Synonyms: absolve, clear, excuse, exonerate

Antonyms: blame, condemn

---

45. Extant [ex-tant]

Adjective
>Still in existence: *Great care must be taken to study extant artifacts of ancient periods.*

Synonyms: alive, existent, living

Antonym: extinct

46. Extraneous [ex-**tra**-ne-ous]

Adjective

External; something coming from without: *We tried to ignore extraneous issues while completing the project.*

Of no consequence; irrelevant: *All extraneous decorations were removed from the tree.*

Related words: *Noun* – extraneousness
              Adverb – extraneously

Synonyms: alien, extrinsic, foreign, peripheral, superfluous

Antonyms: indigenous, integral, intrinsic, native, pertinent, relevant

Language experts estimate that the English language now includes about a million words.

47. Feckless [feck-less]

Adjective
Lacking purpose; careless and irresponsible:
*Brandon's feckless attempts at school cost his
dad a lot of money.*

Related words: *Noun* – fecklessness
                 Adverb – fecklessly

Synonyms: careless, purposeless, useless, valueless

Antonyms: competent, effective, focused,
headstrong, purposeful, responsible, strong,
useful

48. Feign [feign]

Verb
To pretend: *Marilyn feigned an illness so she
would not have to go on the date.*

To imitate in order to deceive: *The caller
feigned the voice of Lucy's teacher.*

Related words: *Noun* – feigner
                 Adverb – feigningly

Synonyms: act, fake, simulate

49. Fractious [frac-tious]

Adjective
> Contentious; difficult; testy: *The minister appealed to those with a fractious spirit to reconsider their attitudes.*

Related words: *Noun* – fractiousness
                  Adverb – fractiously

Synonyms: brittle, contrary, cranky, obstinate, petulant, peevish, snappish, stubborn, touchy

Antonyms: agreeable, amiable, congenial, good-natured, patient

---

50. Hubris [hu-bris]

Noun
> Excessive pride: *The dictator's hubris was ultimately his downfall.*

Related words: *Adjective* – hubristic
                  Adverb – hubristically

**"We've seen the hubris. And now we're seeing the scandals."
- David R. Gergen**

51. Imperative [im-**per**-a-tive]

Adjective
Necessary; unavoidable: *It is imperative that I attend the meeting.*

In grammar, the mood of the verb used to command or request: *Listen!*

Noun
An obligation or duty: *There are certain social imperatives that must be observed.*

Related words: *Noun* – imperativeness
                        Adverb – imperatively

Synonyms: compelling, essential, inescapable, needed, obligatory, required, urgent

Antonyms: discretionary, optional, unnecessary, voluntary

"War is not merely justifiable, but imperative upon honorable men, upon an honorable nation, where peace can only be obtained by the sacrifice of conscientious conviction or of national welfare."
– Theodore Roosevelt

52. Impertinent [im-**per**-ti-nent]

Adjective
   Improperly bold; insolent: *He acted in an impertinent way to his elders.*

Related words: *Noun* – impertinence
                 Adverb – impertinently

Synonyms: arrogant, brazen, disrespectful, insulting, officious, rude

Antonyms: kind, mannered, nice, polite, refined, respectful, submissive

53. Implacable [im-**plac**-a-ble]

Adjective
>Not to be appeased or won over: *We faced implacable opposition on the issue.*

Related words: *Nouns* – implacableness,
>>implacability
>*Adverb* – implacably

Synonyms: rigid, unappeasable, unbending, unmovable

Antonyms: compliant, kind, placable

Readers of Noah Webster's *American Speller* could not only learn new words, they could get instruction on common sense, morals, and good citizenship from the volume.

54. Incorrigible [in-**cor**-ri-gi-ble]

Adjective
>Bad beyond correction: *The child's incorrigible behavior was admitted by his classmates.*

>Firmly fixed: *Celeste has the incorrigible habit of biting her fingernails.*

Noun
>One who cannot be corrected or reformed: *Ned is an incorrigible.*

Related words: *Nouns* – incorrigibility, incorrigibleness
>*Adverb* – incorrigibly

Synonym: unmanageable

Antonyms: compliant, manageable, obedient, reformable, repentant

>**"It gives me great pleasure indeed to see the stubbornness of an incorrigible nonconformist warmly acclaimed."**
>**- Albert Einstein**

55. Incredulous [in-**cred**-u-lous]

Adjective
   Unbelieving; skeptical: *Jared gave us an
   incredulous look when he heard the price of
   the house.*

Related words: *Noun* – incredulousness
                 Adverb – incredulously

Synonyms: doubtful, questioning

Antonyms: believing, convinced, gullible

56. Indigenous [in-**dig**-e-nous]

Adjective

Characteristic of a particular region: *Black bears are indigenous to North Carolina.*

An integral part of: *Larry's sense of humor is indigenous to his personality.*

Related words: *Nouns* – indigenity, indigenousness
Adverb – indigenously

Synonyms: aboriginal, congenital, ingrained, intrinsic, native, natural

Antonyms: alien, foreign

57. Indigent [in-di-gent]

Adjective
> Lacking basic necessities of life because of poverty; needy: *Our church helped the indigent family at Christmas time.*

Noun
> A person that lacks basic necessities: *The indigent was invited inside during freezing weather.*

Related word: *Adverb* – indigently

Synonyms: destitute, impoverished, poor

Antonyms: rich, wealthy

> **"Democracy is when the indigent, and not the men of property, are the rulers."**
> **- Aristotle**

58. Inhibit [in-**hib**-it]

Verb

To restrain, or prohibit: *Please don't let me inhibit your desire for free expression.*

To hold back: *The medicine will inhibit your body's normal signal that you are in pain.*

Related words: *Adjectives* – inhibitable, inhibitive, inhibitory

Synonyms: bridle, conquer, control, curb, constrain, constrict, disallow, discourage, forbid, interdict, limit, muffle, obstruct, prevent, proscribe, repress, restrain, restrict, silence, suppress

Antonyms: allow, encourage, promote

59. Innate [in-**nate**]

Adjective

An integral part of something: *Jerry Lewis has an innate sense of comedic timing.*

Possessing naturally, not through learning: *Wild animals have an innate desire to protect their young.*

Related words: *Noun* – innateness
 Adverb – innately

Synonyms: congenital, inborn, inherent, native, natural

Antonyms: acquired, extraneous, extrinsic, learned

> **"My reading is always about musical biographies. I have an innate interest and passion for that."**
> **- Nina Blackwood**

60. Innocuous [in-**noc**-u-ous]

Adjective

Harmless: *The elixir is simply an innocuous home remedy.*

Unlikely to irritate or offend: *Tony made an innocuous remark about the weather.*

Not interesting; bland: *The theatre group presented an innocuous drama for their fund-raiser.*

Related words: *Nouns* – innocuity, innocuousness
                  Adverb – innocuously

Synonyms: bland, innocent, inoffensive, pedestrian

Antonyms: harmful, offensive, poisonous, threatening

"In this particular case, however mechanical and innocuous it might be at other times, Hepzibah's contortion of brow served her in good stead."
- From *House of Seven Gables* by Nathaniel Hawthorne

61. Innuendo [in-nu-**en**-do]

Noun

A suggestion of information, especially something negative: *Timothy made an inappropriate innuendo about Susan's social life.*

In legal matters, a parenthetical explanation in a pleading: *The innuendo was brief and to the point.*

Also in the law, a plaintiff's interpretation in an action of slander or libel: *Some of the words used in the plaintiff's innuendo were shocking.*

Synonyms: implication, insinuation, reference

"When public men indulge themselves in abuse, when they deny others a fair trial, when they resort to innuendo and insinuation, to libel, scandal, and suspicion, then our democratic society is outraged, and democracy is baffled."
– J. William Fulbright

62. Insipid [in-**sip**-id]

Adjective

Bland; without distinction: *The investigator was an insipid man who drew no attention to his work.*

Not having enough taste to be pleasing, as in food or drink: *Every dish in the meal was more insipid than the one before.*

Related words: *Nouns* – insipidity, insipidness
                       Adverb – insipidly

Synonyms: boring, dull, flat, innocuous, tasteless, vapid

Antonyms: exciting, original, unique, vibrant

> **"To be really great in little things, to be truly noble and heroic in the insipid details of everyday life, is a virtue so rare as to be worthy of canonization."**
> **– Harriet Beecher Stowe**

63. Laconic [la-**con**-ic]

Adjective
> Saying much with a few words; pithy; concise:
> *The father's laconic reply left no doubt that he expected results.*

Related word: *Adverb* – laconically

Synonyms: brief, compact, concise, pithy, terse, succinct

Antonyms: detailed, long, loquacious, long-winded, prolific, verbose, wordy

64. Loquacious [lo-**qua**-cious]

Adjective
   Talkative; wordy: *I had a loquacious roommate on my recent trip.*

Related words: *Nouns* – loquaciousness, loquacity
   Adverb – loquaciously

Synonyms: garrulous, verbose, voluble

Antonyms: laconic, quiet, soft-spoken, subdued, taciturn

> **"He who seldom speaks, and with one calm well-timed word can strike dumb the loquacious, is a genius or a hero."**
> **– Johann Kaspar Lavater**

65. Malevolent [ma-**lev**-o-lent]

Adjective
Showing ill will or wishing harm on others:
Joan's rejected lover made malevolent remarks about her new boyfriend.

Related words: *Noun* – malevolence
                Adverb – malevolently

Synonyms: evil, hateful, malicious, malignant, mean, nasty, venomous, vicious

Antonyms: amiable, benevolent, benign, harmless, kind, loving, warm

66. Misanthrope [mis-an-thrope]

Noun
> One who mistrusts or hates mankind: *The home of the town's misanthrope was as isolated as the man himself.*

Related words: *Noun* – misanthropy
    Adverb – misanthropically

Synonyms: cynic, recluse

Antonyms: humanitarian, philanthropist

Noam Chomsky estimated that there are about 500,000 descriptive rules for any language that a speaker has to know about word order, pronunciation, word formation, and sentence structure before he can be a fluent speaker of a language.

67. Misnomer [mis-**no**-mer]

Noun
> Misnamed: *To call that group of buildings a town is a misnomer.*

Related word: *Adjective* – misnomered

> "The 'environmental crisis' is a misnomer, since it is (of course) a crisis of ourselves, not of the environment."
> – Wendell Berry

68. Misogynist [mi-**sog**-y-nist]

Noun
> One who hates women: *David's unfortunate romantic history made him a confirmed misogynist.*

Related words: *Noun* – misogyny
> *Adjectives* – misogynic, misogynistic, misogynous

69. Mitigate [mit-i-gate]

Verb

To lessen in intensity; to dilute: *Bob's anger was mitigated by the kind words expressed by his opponent.*

To make less severe: *Consequences of the crime were mitigated by the circumstances.*

Related words:　*Nouns* – mitigation, mitigator
　　　　　　　　Adjectives – mitigable, mitigative, mitigatory
　　　　　　　　Adverb – mitigatedly

Synonyms: allay, alleviate, assuage, ease, lighten, relieve

Antonyms: aggravate, incite, increase, intensify, irritate, worsen

"To rejoice in another's prosperity is to give content to your lot; to mitigate another's grief is to alleviate or dispel your own."
- Tryon Edwards

70. Narcissism [**nar**-cis-sism]

Noun

Excessive self-love; vanity: *Self-respect is healthy; narcissism can make you unpleasant to be around.*

A psychological condition characterized by self-preoccupation: *His narcissism made it difficult for Paul to maintain a romantic relationship.*

Related words: *Noun* – narcissist
               Adjective – narcissistic
               Adverb – narcissistically

Synonyms: conceit, egocentrism, pride, self-centeredness, vanity

Antonyms: self-effacing, self-loathing

**"Shyness has a strange element of narcissism, a belief that how we look, how we perform, is truly important to other people."
- Andre Dubus**

71. Nefarious [ne-**far**-i-ous]

Adjective
> Very wicked: *His nefarious ways were*
> *eventually his downfall.*

Related words: *Noun* – nefariousness
                 Adverb – nefariously

Synonyms: atrocious, heinous, infamous, vile

Antonyms: good, positive

> **"I want them to see that there is life after tragedy, after nefarious notoriety, and see that you can hold your head up."**
> **– Linda Tripp**

72. Obligatory [o-**blig**-a-to-ry]

Adjective

Required; mandatory: *Edward made an obligatory appearance at the reception.*

Out of obligation; incumbent on; *His obligatory praise of Jane's work seemed to appease her.*

Related words: *Noun* – obligatoriness
                  Adverb – obligatorily

Synonyms: compulsory, essential, imperative, necessary, required, requisite

Antonyms: nonessential, optional, voluntary

73. Obsequious [ob-**se**-qui-ous]

Adjective

Exhibiting an overly-compliant attitude; fawning: *The job applicant gave an obsequious smile and comments when he was introduced.*

Attempting to gain favor by flattery; ingratiating: *His obsequious attention to Mr. Brown's children seemed forced.*

Related words: *Noun* – obsequiousness
Adverb – obsequiously

Synonyms: fawning, menial, servile, subservient

Antonyms: arrogant, assertive, boorish, brazen, disrespectful, domineering, presumptuous, rude

74. Panacea [pan-a-**ce**-a]

Noun

A remedy for; a solution for all problems or difficulties: *Pauline thought marriage would be a panacea to all her problems.*

Related word: *Adjective* – panacean

Synonyms: balm, cure, elixir

Antonym: irritant

Origin: In mythology, Panacea was the ancient Greek goddess of healing.

More than 750 million people speak English—about 380 million of those use it as their primary language.

75. Paucity [pau-ci-ty]

Noun
>Lack or shortage of; a small or inadequate number: *There was a paucity of qualified candidates for the office.*

Synonyms: dearth, deficiency, deficit, inadequacy, lack, scarceness, shortage, shortfall

Antonyms: abundance, affluence, bounty, excess, overflow, plenty

---

76. Peccadillo [pec-ca-**dil**-lo]

Noun
>A minor or slight offense; a small fault: *Mr. Simpson's indiscretion was called a peccadillo in the newspaper article.*

Related words: *Noun* – peccadilloes *or* peccadillos (*plural*)

Synonyms: faux pas, indiscretion, sin

77. Pedantic [pe-**dan**-tic]

Adjective
Overly concerned with details or trivial formalisms: *Keith displayed a pedantic attention to details without seeing the big picture.*

Related words: *Noun* – pedanticalness
                 Adverb – pedantically

Synonyms: academic, bookish, formalistic, legalistic

Antonyms: carefree, imprecise, informal, loose

"A good designer must rely on experience, on precise, logic thinking; and on pedantic exactness. No magic will do."
– Niklaus Wirth

78. Penchant [pen-chant]

Noun

A strong preference for: *The James family has a penchant for strong coffee.*

Likely to do: *He has a penchant for coming in late for meetings.*

Synonyms: bent, bias, fondness, predilection, predisposition, proclivity, proneness, propensity, tendency, turn

Antonyms: dislike, hatred, indifference

"I have learned that there lies dormant in the souls of all men a penchant for some particular musical instrument, and an unsuspected yearning to learn to play on it, that are bound to wake up and demand attention some day."
- From "A Touching Story of George Washington's Boyhood" by Mark Twain

79. Peripheral [pe-**riph**-er-al]

Adjective

Surrounding or external; relatively minor: *The committee spent more time on peripheral issues than on the items on the agenda.*

In anatomy, the surface or outer part of a body or organ: *The lab session focused on the peripheral nervous system.*

In computer science, auxiliary devices such as a printer that work in conjunction with the computer.

Related words: *Noun* – periphery
                 Adverb – peripherally

Synonym: outside

Antonyms: center, heart, indigenous, inherent, internal, middle

80. Pejorative [pe-**jo**-ra-tive]

Noun

A negative word meant to demean: *The speech included a pejorative that was not well received by the audience.*

Adjective

Belittling or negative: *The press used a pejorative term for the young man on trial.*

Related word: *Adverb* – pejoratively

Synonyms: belittling, deprecatory, disparaging

Antonyms: complimentary, praise

"The pejorative term 'political correctness' was adapted to express disapproval of the enlargement of etiquette to cover all people, in spite of this being a principle to which all Americans claim to subscribe."
- Judith S. Marin

81. Peruse [pe-**rus**e]

Verb

> To read thoroughly: *Please peruse the document and send a response as soon as possible.*

Related words: *Nouns* – perusal, peruser
                     Adjective – perusable

Synonyms: check, examine, go over, inspect, review, scrutinize, study

Antonyms: glance, overlook, scan, skim

82. Petulant [pet-u-lant]

Adjective
Irritated or impatient; ill-tempered; easily
annoyed: *The professor's petulant response to
the question took us all by surprise.*

Related words: *Nouns* – petulance, petulancy
                 Adverb – petulantly

Synonyms: bad-tempered, cantankerous, crabby,
    cranky, cross, disagreeable, fretful, grumpy, ill-
    tempered, irascible, irritable, nasty, peevish,
    snappy, surly, touchy, ugly

Antonyms: affable, easy going, good-humored,
    good-natured, happy, pleasant

83. Placate [**pla**-cate]

Verb

To pacify; to appease: *Mayor Griffin tried to appease the angry group of citizens.*

Related words: *Nouns* – placater, placation
                Adjectives – placative, placatory

Synonyms: assuage, calm, conciliate, mollify, satisfy, soothe

Antonyms: agitate, anger, annoy, irritate, provoke, upset, worry

---

The longest English word to appear in standard English dictionaries is: pneumonoultramicroscopicsilicovolcanokoniosis (45 letters). This is the name of a lung disease suffered by miners.

84. Plethora [pleth-o-ra]

Noun

An excess; an overabundance: *We had a plethora of applicants for the job.*

In pathology, an excess of blood in one organ or area of the body.

Related word: *Adjective* – plethoric

Synonyms: plenty, sufficiency

Antonyms: dearth, lack, paucity, rarity, scarcity

85. Preclude [pre-**clude**]

Verb
>To exclude; to make exempt; to make impossible: *His lack of certification precluded his being eligible for the job.*

Related words: *Noun* – preclusion
                     Adjectives – precludable, preclusive
                     Adverb – preclusively

Synonyms: avert, eliminate, forestall, prevent, ward off

Antonyms: allow, encourage, permit, promote, support

> **"Relationships do not preclude issues of morality."**
> **– Jhumpa Lahiri**

86. Precursor [pre-**cur**-sor]

Noun

A person or thing that comes before something else and indicates that something else is coming: *The change in directors was a precursor to other changes in administration.*

In chemistry, a chemical that is transformed into another compound during a chemical reaction so that its previous identity precedes the new one: *The textbook said that cholesterol is a precursor of testosterone.*

In biology, a cell or tissue that gives rise to a more mature form: *The precursor of the substance could not immediately be identified.*

Synonyms: ancestor, forerunner, foreshadower, harbinger, herald, presager

Antonyms: descendant, follower, successor

> "*Life* magazine ran a page featuring me and three other girls that was clearly the precursor of *Sports Illustrated* swimsuit issues."
> – Esther Williams

87. Prolific [pro-**lif**-ic]

Adjective

Producing in large quantities: *John Grisham is a prolific author.*

Highly fruitful: *The pear trees were prolific this year.*

Related words: *Nouns* – prolificacy, prolificness
Adverb – prolifically

Synonyms: abundant, fecund, fertile, productive, teeming

Antonyms: barren, fruitless, impotent, unfruitful, unproductive

"Debt is a prolific mother of folly and crime."
–   Benjamin Disraeli

88. Quintessential
[quin-tes-**sen**-tial]

Adjective
>A nearly perfect embodiment of a thing or
>ideal: *He was the quintessential gentleman.*

Related words: *Noun* – quintessence
>>>>*Adverb* – quintessentially

Synonyms: archetypal, archetypical, classic, model,
>paradigmatic, prototypal, prototypical,
>representative, typical

Antonyms: atypical, unique

89. Salacious [sa-la-cious]

Adjective
Lustful or bawdy: *The director did not mind that the play had a salacious theme.*

Related words: *Noun* – salaciousness, salacity
                     Adverb – salaciously

Synonyms: erotic, indecent, lascivious, lecherous, lewd, obscene, pornographic

Antonyms: decent, modest

Despite numerous attempts from several parties, the United States does not recognize English as its official language, but it has been adopted by about half of the individual states.

90. Solicitous [so-**lic**-i-tous]

Adjective

Anxious or concerned: *He was a solicitous parent during his child's illness.*

Expressing concern: *Jackie was solicitous during our trying time.*

Eager: *He was always a solicitous employee.*

Extremely careful: *The minister was solicitous with his behavior.*

Related words: *Noun* – solicitousness
                 Adverb – solicitously

Synonyms: attentive, mindful, worried

Antonyms: careless, easy-going, laid-back, unconcerned

"I am not solicitous to examine particularly everything here, which indeed could not be done in fifty years, because my desire is to make all possible discoveries, and return to your Highnesses, if it please our Lord, in April."
– Christopher Columbus

91. Specious [spe-cious]

Adjective
> Seeming to be good, but lacking substance: *His specious words were carefully chosen.*

> Deceptively attractive: *Susan had no clue about his specious behavior.*

Related words: *Nouns* – speciousness, speciosity
                 Adverb – speciously

Synonyms: fallacious, false, insincere, invalid, misleading, shallow, spurious

Antonyms: genuine, legitimate, real, solid, substantive, true, valid

> **"A thing may look specious in theory, and yet be ruinous in practice."**
> **– Edmond Burke**

92. Succinct [suc-**cinct**]

Adjective

Expressed clearly in few words: *Larry's explanation of the dilemma was succinct and clear.*

Compressed into a small area: *All of the camper's necessities were put in a succinct bundle.*

Related words: *Noun* – succinctness
                 Adverb – succinctly

Synonyms: compendious, concise, laconic, lean, terse

Antonyms: long-winded, rambling, unstructured, verbose, wordy

93. Suffrage [suf-frage]

Noun

The right to vote: *It is hard to believe that women's suffrage was ever in question.*

A short intercessory prayer: *Rev. Sanders offered a suffrage before the service began.*

94. Tacit [tac-it]

Adjective

Implied; understood without being said: *The two partners gave tacit approval of the project before it began.*

Silent: *Mr. Lee was a tacit partner in the company.*

Unspoken: *We all offered a tacit prayer for the child's safety.*

Related words: *Noun* – tacitness
                 Adverb – tacitly

Synonyms: implicit, silent, unexpressed, unsaid, unvoiced, wordless

Antonyms: explicit, expressed

"Culture is the tacit agreement to let the means of a subsistence disappear behind the purpose of existence."
– Karl Kraus

95. Tenacious [te-**na**-cious]

Adjective

Holding firm: *Matthew's hold on the rope was tenacious.*

Not easily torn asunder: *The group had quickly formed a tenacious bond.*

Related words: *Nouns* – tenaciousness, tenacity
                 Adverb – tenaciously

Synonyms: clinging, dogged, firm, obstinate, strong, pigheaded, secure, strong-willed, unrelenting, willful

Antonyms: flexible, loose, slack, surrendering, weak, yielding

> "I believe that if you have real talent as a writer, a true gift, you will eventually be published. But it may not happen according to your schedule. And it may not happen with the first manuscript you create. Or the second. So you have to be, if not patient, at least endlessly tenacious."
> – Augusten Burroughs

96. Trite [trite]

Adjective

Ineffective because of overuse: *The mayor's trite speech fell on deaf ears.*

Lacking substance or originality: *His trite excuses had become commonplace.*

Related words: *Noun* – triteness
Adverb – tritely

Synonyms: commonplace, hackneyed, ordinary, stale, unoriginal

Antonyms: important, impressive, original, significant, substantive

> **"It is by vivacity and wit that man shines in company; but trite jokes and loud laughter reduce him to a buffoon."**
> **- Lord Chesterfield**

97. Ubiquitous [u-**biq**-ui-tous]

Adjective
Existing everywhere, often at the same time:
*We saw the ubiquitous fast food chains even
when we traveled abroad.*

Related words: *Noun* – ubiquitousness
                 Adverb – ubiquitously

Synonyms: ever-present, omnipresent, universal

Antonyms: rare, restricted, scarce

"Outside of the chair, the teapot is
the most ubiquitous and important
design element in the domestic
environment and almost everyone
who has tackled the world of design
has ended up designing one."
– David McFadden

98. Verbose [ver-**bose**]

Adjective
Wordy; using an excessive number of words:
Sonny was a quiet man, but his wife was verbose.

Related words: *Nouns* – verboseness, verbosity
                    Adverb – verbosely

Synonyms: long-winded, loquacious, prolific, talkative

Antonyms: concise, laconic, succinct, terse

99. Voracious [vo-**ra**-cious]

Adjective

Consuming large quantities of food: *George has a voracious appetite.*

Eager or avid: *Becky is a voracious reader.*

Related words: *Nouns* – voraciousness, voracity
Adverb – voraciously

Synonyms: greedy, insatiable, rapacious, ravenous

Antonyms: disinterested, limited, poor, satisfied

> **"Ego has a voracious appetite, the more you feed it, the hungrier it gets."**
> **– Nathaniel Bronner Jr.**

100. Wary [war-y]

Adjective

Being on guard against danger: *Children should always be wary of strangers.*

Cautious: *He gave us a wary look when he heard the loud thunder.*

Related words: *Noun* – wariness
Adverb – warily

Synonyms: alert, aware, guarded, prudent, skeptical, vigilant, watchful

Antonyms: open, vulnerable

"Be wary of the man who urges an action in which he himself incurs no risk."
- Seneca

101. Winnow [win-now]

Verb

To separate the chaff from grain with air: *The farmer showed the children how to winnow the wheat from the chaff.*

To extract undesirable parts: *We tried to winnow the legitimate points from the useless material in the report.*

To blow on: *I watched the wind winnow the child's cornsilk hair.*

Related words: *Noun* – winnower
                 Verbs – winnowed, winnowing, winnows

Synonyms: set apart, separate, sort, sift

Antonyms: combine, include

> **"We shall be winnow'd with so rough a wind**
>
> **That even our corn shall seem as light as chaff**
>
> **And good from bad find no partition."**
>
> **- From *Henry IV, Part 2* by William Shakespeare**